Things to Say in the Dark

By Miriam Moss

DORRANCE
PUBLISHING CO
EST. 1920
PITTSBURGH, PENNSYLVANIA 15238

Dorrance Publishing Co
585 Alpha Drive
Pittsburgh, PA 15238
Visit our website at *www.dorrancebookstore.com*

ISBN: 979-8-88683-388-1
eISBN: 979-8-88683-367-6

Things to Say in the Dark

Space

Space;
You said you needed space so I created galaxies for you
Where you could collect as many stars as you wanted.
I created nebulas and auroras for you to look at
When you got tired of counting constellations,
And I made a sun so you'd stay cozy while you're there.
Never once did it cross my mind
That for some unfathomable reason
You meant space from me.
And once again I become too much to handle,
Just for someone else because that's what I do,
I overflow until I've ruined the table
And made a mess I can't clean up.
Instead of giving you space, I gave you space;
And I guess that explains why you never told me
That I have stars in my eyes
Because I handed them all to you first,
And when love sent me to the moon
I waited there for you, but you never came.
I hope it feels lonely out there.
I hope a black hole comes and swallows you up
Along with everything I ever gave you.
I hope it's cold, and dark, and scary all the time.
But in a strange way, you still got what you wanted.

And I can't even be mad at you really
Because it's not your fault I do this.
But I hate how dull my eyes are now
And I hate how I ruined the best parts of me
Ruining the best parts of you.
Maybe if we're lucky
A meteor will take us out like the dinosaurs
But I never get lucky as you well know.
So I just have to sit in this void I made,
Surrounded by this infinite emptiness all the time
Because you never flew up here too.

Collecting Memories

I wish I could collect memories like my brother collects movies.
Able to pull you off a shelf anytime I wanted
And watch what we went through over and over again.
It's the only way I'll remember any of it happened.
I wish I could press pause and play and rewind
So I only have to live through what I want.
Instead, I think I collect memories like he collects action figures;
Probably not as much as anyone else would assume,
And I leave you all on a shelf just the same,
Doing nothing as the dust settles in.
It's funny how my only fear is oblivion,
Yet that's exactly what I doom everyone in my life to
Because I'm too scared of getting lost in the past.
Life isn't a movie and my recollection of it isn't the scenes that get
    the cut.
Life hurts and it doesn't always get a happy ending,
So I just avoid the bad scenes even if it's most of them.
I'm sorry if your character got written out or fired,
But I can't fast-forward to a time where you didn't disappoint me
And if I'm the main character, why would I want that around?
I'm forgetful because I want to be
And my collection is small because I only bother sticking with my
    favorites.
It's hardly a real collection, I'm well aware,
But it's really the only things I need.
And I make sure to dust those off.

22

Nobody warned me that high school would suddenly feel like a
  lifetime ago by the time I would turn 22.
And how love is so cruel that he should have been a groom, but
  now I feel guilty 'cause instead I miss you.

Nothing lasts forever; I've made a habit of thinking that it will.
And if I'm always bottled up it only makes a bigger spill.
'Cause friends, they lie, and people die, and no matter how they
  leave it hurts the same.
Or when everything's fucked sometimes it sucks 'cause no one is
  to blame.

Made a promise to a boy that we'd stay friends, now we don't speak.
Is it the mood swings or the drugs, or was yesterday last week?
Everything's changed and it feels like my brain might explode at
  any time.
And my mom likes to hit but she won't admit when she crossed the
  line.

I'm drowning in oceans and already I almost didn't make it past
  the lakes.
All I like is sleeping but I'm always wide awake.
Always had tunnel vision but now it feels more like a bridge,
'Cause if I don't keep looking forward it might make me run off
  the edge.
Take it day by day, they say, but what if every day feels heavier
  than before?
'Cause I've stayed the same but there's no way I am who I was before.

Stardust

I'm scared that I don't love you.
I'm scared that you cannot be my jar of stardust,
But rather just a jar of dirt or some glitter.
I'm scared that I will kiss her
And feel more sparks than I do with you.
Because we are not the sky when it explodes in July,
We are but a bag of pop-its.
We are melting water, though we used to be solid.
I'm sorry I cannot give to you,
Although to be fair, you've given me more than it's worth.
I've tried many times to fight this,
But the gifts only make it worse.
I cannot tell you that you complete me
Because no part of me was missing before.
My soul was all still there,
And confidence is rich, but I am poor.
I'm angry at the Gods
Who made you think you belong to me.
Maybe I'm just a realist, or maybe it's a pessimist,
But I can't find the sense in what that means.
I'm scared of letting you think that you are my moon
When indeed you do not light up my darkest hour.
I am your whole garden; you are but my one flower.
I'm scared that I don't love you.
And I don't want to hurt you,
But band aids have got to be ripped off.

I'm sorry I was your butterfly and you were only my moth.
No one knows what to tell me to make the pain fade.
Sometimes the person you are yesterday
Is not that same person today.
And I'm debating if you mean a lot to me,
Or if maybe it's just common courtesy.
My paper won't give me answers,
So at least it's making me come clean.
I'm scared that I don't love you,
And that it will break your heart.
I'm scared of leaving you for her
Because I'm also scared of starts.
So I will not tell you that I love you,
Because I've never been able to perfect my poker face,
And I don't want to disguise the truth behind a lie.
I don't want to try and hide a monster behind these eyes.
I don't think I love you.
But you are all that I have, so still I hold on.
And maybe it's wrong,
But it sure felt like the stars were falling at first.
The pressure was crushing, but everything lit up so beautifully.
I tried to collect the moon's fireflies, but then it only got worse.
I guess when I was scraping up the sky
The dirt mixed in with it too.
You wanted fast, but I could only go slow
And that was when I realized
Stars died long ago.

Regret

You'd think I'd hate myself for giving you all of me.
And I thought you'd be more sorry after I gave you my body.
And it's funny how I run in circles around my head,
Trying to understand why you did what you did.
'Cause I put up with you though it was rough,
And you relied on me not calling out your bluff.
And I hate that I thought it was love,
But the only thing that I regret
Is not being enough.

Valentine's Day

Yesterday was Valentine's Day
And I wanted to write you a card.
But remembering you'll never read it
Made it extra hard.

It would've said I love you,
Forever and to the moon.
It's brighter than the sun
And stronger than a monsoon.

It's as endless as the universe,
It's deeper than the sea.
It's warmer than the summer,
As constant as gravity.

It's a promise and a truth,
It's a poem and a song,
Though it always sounded better
When you used to sing along.

It breaks my heart to miss you
And know I won't see you soon.
So until that day, I love you,
Forever and to the moon.

Tylenol

You said not talking to me would kill you
But it's starting to look like it's killing you in the way a bad
    headache does
And not in the way that your breath would catch in your throat
    every time you expected fresh air.

I mean, I don't literally want you to die,
But if I had known that all it took was an over-the-counter,
Take two pills from your bathroom cabinet and you'll be fine type
    of cure,
I sure wouldn't have wasted my time thinking I meant so much to
    you.

Non/Suicidal Thoughts

I dig holes for myself then complain when the dirt starts to bury me.
Wanting to die and not wanting to live are two very different things
Even if society treats them both the same.
I'd dig my grave way before I'm ready to jump in it
Just to have the option if I change my mind,
But that doesn't mean I want to suffocate while I wait.
It's hard enough to breathe as is.
I have a problem of creating problems
Then abandoning everything when nothing works out.
I am an enigma to even myself
And figuring out the root of my self-loathing
Has taken my whole life thus far.
I am not afraid to admit I like the attention,
But I wish I didn't feel the need to be reassured by it
To prove someone cared after all.
I am composed of all the broken and ugly parts of my mother,
And every ray of sunshine and happiness that has seeped into my soul.
A perfect yin yang of hatred and beauty
That I try so hard to make a full circle out of instead.
No, I'm not scared of dying,
But I'm scared of death itself.
What-if's cloud my mind
And that is why I say I'm not suicidal,
Because I doubt I'll ever commit to the idea of the unknown.
Of permanence, because my lows and highs always come in cycles.
I cannot trust a brain that tells me to kill myself
If it's the same brain that preaches self-care possibly a week later.
There's been lots of days where I don't want to live
But I hardly ever want to die.

Gone

You left a hole in me.
A hole the size of Texas and my body was just Rhode Island.
I am not just incomplete, I am obliterated.
Skin heals but the heart doesn't.
I find myself missing you in the most random parts of the day—
Driving home from work,
Singing with a friend,
Going on a walk.
Things that should still be the same without you just aren't.
Because you didn't just die, you changed my whole world.
And when the world keeps spinning when mine has stood still,
I begin to wonder if I'll ever catch up to reality again.
I miss you.
That's all there is to it; I miss you.
I wish I could say more, but my brain is numb from feeling already
And if time has stopped anyway, then why bother with anything
    else?
Until the sky turns green,
Until the flowers don't bloom,
Until the waves stop crashing,
Until the sun stops rising,
Until my own last breath,
I miss you.

Soulmates Somewhere Else

I heard someone once say,
"It's a different type of pain to be soulmates but not in love."
If you'd asked my younger self,
I wouldn't even say that was possible.
But meeting you, I'd felt like I already knew you.
I felt comfortable in a way I never have been before.
Gravity pulled us together like a cosmic sign from the universe,
So why didn't it work?
We fit like puzzle pieces
But it wasn't a good picture.
And I wanted so badly for you to be "the one"
That I didn't care if the picture was ugly.
That's not how love works though.
Love is supposed to make things beautiful,
Not just fit into place.
I'll always believe you were my soulmate,
And I'll always hate it wasn't more than that.
If I died a thousand times,
I hope our paths still cross in a couple different lives.
I'm confident we got it right in at least one.

The Art of Almost

"Jack of all trades, master of none,"
But I have mastered the art of "almost."
Almost running away,
Almost reaching my dream,
Almost getting married;
No one has had as many "almost's" as me.
And second best is fine,
But after a while you start to wonder
If it's even worth trying if you know the end result.
Holding your hand was nice
Until your fingers slipped through mine
Like I knew was bound to happen.
I still get my hopes too high every time
So every "almost" crushes me with the weight of a mountain
Because I can't learn to expect less than what I want.
Almost moved out,
Almost got the role,
Almost had grades just as good as my siblings;
I'm always the runner-up
And never the winning contestant.
Above average,
Yet far below superior.
Everyone says it's better to be a jack of all trades,
But I'd do anything to be special at something.

15

To only want to do one thing
Instead of focusing on everything
And always coming up short because of it.
There's not a fiber of my being that excels in anything.
I'm pretty but not gorgeous,
I'm athletic but not an athlete,
I'm smart but not a genius,
I'm not anything but "almost."

Phantom Limb

They say you can't lose what you never had,
But that's not true because you lose all the chances and possibili-
    ties of what could have been.
You were never mine,
Yet I definitely lost something
And it hurt like hell.
Like phantom limb pains from people born without them to begin
    with.
Yeah, you didn't lose anything,
But something was still missing.
You feel like a phantom limb.
A part of me that should've still been there.
I only knew life without you before
So tell me why I'm getting the sensation that our hands should be
    touching
When they never did to begin with.
Although there's nothing there to be hurt over,
I am.
Maybe it wasn't losing you,
So much as it was losing myself.
I gave you a part of me that I don't think I'm ever getting back.
Sometimes I wonder if you feel it too.
If I took something from you as well.
Would you say you lost me?
Do you think you even had me?

Jacket

Last time I wore my heart on my sleeve
It broke into a million pieces
So now I make sure to wear a jacket.
You asked me once
How I can manage to wear that
In the summer heat
And I simply responded by saying,
"I like how it looks."
But that's not true
And I'm endlessly dying
Waiting on the time and place
To openly show affection again.
The coat hanger by my door
And closet in my room
Beg to have someone over,
Yearn to show someone the shards
In hopes that maybe they could fix it.
And maybe in private
The jacket can be taken off
To remind myself I at least still have a heart at all.
Maybe in private
It's not so scary to tell the world it can break you.
Maybe in private,
At least if it breaks,
It's only one person at a time.

Spare Change

The moment you left me I knew it was forever.
Still, I spent my life denying it
Because how could we go through what we did
Just for you to end it all in a day?
The summer before I left,
I was worried to death
Because something gave me the sense
That I'd never be in your house again.
I just didn't know I'd be right.
My brain knew you were gone
Long before my heart did.
Still, I kept you around
Like spare change in my pocket
That I might pull out again.
I outgrew those jeans
Long before I took them off
Because I'd hoped so badly they would fit again
But all I did was spend a really long time
Feeling uncomfortable and ugly instead.
You don't care.
You threw me out and discarded me
The second you realized I was less than $20.
You wouldn't keep me around if I was a crumpled $5,
Let alone the leftovers like I did,
Especially after you spent me on her.

I can still hear the jingling of coins,
And my fingers are stained green
After holding on for so long.
The spare change I used to collect in jars
From couch cushions and tips
Has all been tainted now
With the memory and association of you.
Everything has been really.
If I'm being totally honest
I see you still in everything.
And after all this time,
If you told me today that you would change for me,
I'd spare you the argument that we should probably have
Because I want you back so badly.
I miss the weight of you on my side.
I miss the style of jeans I outgrew.
I miss feeling richer—
Even if I truly wasn't,
I felt it just because the pennies and dimes were so significant.
I miss the jingling that still echoes inside my head.
But most of all,
I miss you.

Russian Roulette

I played Russian roulette with a BB gun
Just for fun
To see who would care if it was real.
Put a shot through my head,
But I'm not dead,
Just made it hurt so I knew I could feel.
'Cause they'll all scream
If the walls ain't clean,
And they're splattered with blood instead.
But the bruises can hide
So they'll tell me I'm fine,
But I still put a gun to my head.

Untitled I

I always pictured y'all being there on my wedding day.
And maybe you would've if I hadn't run away.
Told too many people that I wish I would've stayed.

I'll drink a glass and convince myself I'll wake up somewhere better.
But morning always comes and whiskey tastes too bitter.
No matter how I try and forget, it's something I'll remember.

'Cause I lost everyone I loved in less than a year,
But my therapist just tells me it's anxiety and fear.
And no one has to make me feel bad,
I already do that to myself.
My self-sabotage always lets it get too bad
Before I ever ask for help.

This house is lonely for the first time since 1962.
My aunt's been moving on, but I know she feels it too.
Three months is a long time to not know what to do.

And he's still looking for a girl ever since I let him down.
I've worn black too many times instead of a white gown.
This city keeps on growing, but it's a smaller town.

'Cause I lost everyone I loved in less than a year,
And plans all fall apart so now I play it just by ear.
And no one can make me feel worse
Than I already always do.
'Cause I'm the one who hurt y'all,
But I'm the one that wears the bruise.

No flowers in my hand, just flowers on two graves.
I know how to swim, but tsunamis aren't just waves.
If I believed in God before, there's no way that I would now.
Just when I hit rock bottom, the ground somehow gives out.

'Cause I lost everyone I loved in less than a year,
And it's surprising to myself that I'm still even here.
I drink and smoke it all away,
Though I know it's bad for my health.
And no one has to make me feel bad,
I already do that to myself.

Untitled II

I'm trying to write of love
Like I remember when it was mine.
When I thought
Wildflowers grew for the sole purpose
Of braiding them in your hair,
Or when I couldn't watch a sunset
Without taking a picture to send to you.
Love was wasting all our time together
Because we knew everything is pointless
But it made the time we had worth something.
It was telling secrets in the dark
And wiping tears when they
Became too hard to say out loud.
The intimacy of touching scars
In places no one else would be allowed to see.
Journal entries we would never exchange
Just because you were on my mind
And I wanted to express
What I could never say.
Love was shown in the little things,
The hidden gestures we'd make
When we didn't actually want to call it love.
Always saying "goodnight" and "good morning,"
And remembering the way I liked my coffee,
And the way you didn't at all.

24

It was the comfortable silence
And the endless need to be close.
It was when you made sure to kiss my knees
Every time before you put the bandage on.
Ah yes, I remember when love was mine,
Like the pleasant, nostalgic memory
Of my favorite ice cream place as a kid
That is no longer there.
You are a ghost to me now,
But the foundation I am built on.
And though it's something that passes by
But is hardly ever kept,
I remember.

My Body

The first time I let a boy touch me
I was well past 21,
But it's not the first time they did.
My body has been marked
With invisible scars all over
From the ones who touched me first.
In elementary school when a friend
Tried to trap me in his bathroom and lift my shirt;
My neck and chest
From my best friend's ex
When he grabbed me in the hallway at school and bit my neck;
My thighs and worse
From the guy who molested me
In the backseat while my friends were driving up front.
It's no wonder I took so long to open up
Physically and emotionally.
So when the second time I let a boy touch me and more,
And he dropped me off the face of the Earth,
I began to wonder
If a man could ever leave flowers on my body
Instead of burning them all away.
I still don't know the answer
And in truth, I don't care to find out.
If a neighborhood is notoriously known for being robbed
Would you decide to live there?

Sure, it might not happen,
But is it a chance you're willing to take?
My body truly is a temple
Though I have hardly any valuables anymore,
So it's hard to trust anyone else
To keep them protected at all costs.
There's good people,
I know it,
And I'm not ready to give up on that belief.
My trust issues tell me otherwise,
But I know that's just the part of me
That wants to make sure I'm safe.
I have built this temple too high
To be torn down brick by brick
Until someone finds the piece to make it crumble.
My body is mine before it's anybody else's
And I refuse to share residence
Possibly ever again.

Dirty Laundry

Most days I feel like the dirty laundry
That is piled on my bedroom floor.
Not bothered enough to be washed,
But liked too much to be donated.
Sometimes I'll get moved to the laundry basket
And think everything's about to change,
But mostly I end up sitting there
For another period of time.
I long to be washed-
To be clean and spun out of
Every stain and smell
That might remain
If I'm left too much longer.
To be tucked away comfortably
And reassured I could be worn again soon.
Most days I can ignore the fading print,
The thread starting to come undone at the sleeve.
It's proof I was a favorite at some point.
It's proof I was cherished at my best.
And you'll buy new clothes,
I'm well aware,
That you'll like better
Simply because you've grown and changed.
I can't get mad at that; I'm not.

28

I understand that after spending a season in a box
A lot can change
And others might be bought instead.
But at my best, I'm the one you packed in your suitcase,
I'm the one you wore to your first college party,
I'm the one you wanted to put a jacket over
Instead of covering me up with a sweatshirt.
At my best you kept me clean.
But now most days I feel like dirty laundry.

Moon

I am not always comforted by the fact
We all share the same moon.
You don't deserve to see
The way it glows and shimmers
In perfect summer nights.
The crescent shapes and
Pink tinted clouds
Are meant for me and my eyes only.
I let you keep everything else,
But the moon is mine
And I will not allow you
To gaze at it
With amazement in your eyes
As if you are not the darkness
It is trying to outshine.
We may be connected
By its presence and its pull,
But only in the same way
We are connected to the Earth itself.
Soil stretching across the land,
Our footprints once overlapped
But now I am standing in sand
And you are on red clay.

And when I'm farther away even,
There will come a time
When I will always see the moon first
And you will be the one waiting instead.
You might think it looks pretty
But it will always be prettier where I am
Because I'm the type of soul
That makes you appreciate the moon
While you simply look at it.
You don't get to keep me
By reminding yourself
I'm still under the same sky.
I will board your windows
And lock your doors
Before I ever let that happen.
I will let you be the sun
Since you already burn
Everyone that gets too close
So long as it reassures the fact
We will never share the moon again.

This is Me Being Honest

It's not fair of me
To write as if I am always the victim.
I am mean and ugly
Down to my bones
And I've broken
Far too many people
Who have dared to come close.
The same mouth
That utters sweet sentences,
Has also raised her voice
To remind people
How little she cares about them.
I have given up on people
Who would give up the world for me,
Then have the audacity
To sit here and complain
About how there's no one left that's good.
I'm sharp where others curve,
Often cutting those
Who try their best to be gentle.
A fire that keeps herself warm
At the expense of burning everyone close.
I have held and hit
With the same hand before.

32

Have made sure someone is crying
Before I leave the room.
And the worst part is
The remorse comes later,
If it ever comes at all.
I can't seem to make myself
Apologize to certain people.
I refuse to accept
Not everything is
Because of my mother's hate;
Some of it is just who I am.
I can use pity
To manipulate people
Into feeling bad
For why I reacted the way I did.
I loathe myself.
And I'm also my best friend.

Metamorphosis

Of course they all want to talk about
How we will grow into butterflies
When our cocoons make it feel like the end.
That's it; that's the metaphor:
Change will make us into something beautiful.
They never bother to mention how delicate we become.
How now they have to be gentle
Because the slightest wrong touch
Can rip our wings beyond repair.
Not to mention our lifespan
Is now likely much shorter.
And I don't want to be beautiful when I change anyway,
I want to be stronger.
I want to be ready when another unsuspected storm comes,
Not blown away or hiding out.
I think it's a lovely idea
With good intentions
To remind us that this is not the end.
However, what they fail to realize
Is that caterpillars decide when to transform themselves
And often we are shoved into it without any warning.
What they fail to realize
Is that it's lonely waiting in our cocoon to open.
And most importantly there was never anything wrong
With being a caterpillar to begin with.

So I'm here to tell you today
That you are not a butterfly, that you never will be.
You are simply you:
Strong, resilient, loveable, compassionate you
Who didn't change your whole life
Just to be beautiful.

The Guilt of a Granddaughter

Sometimes I feel guilty for living through a life
When I told you I wouldn't be able to go on without you.
Sometimes I'll catch myself caught up in little moments again,
Laughing and smiling like I used to,
Then quickly stop when reality sinks back in
And I have to remind myself
That there's nothing to be happy about anymore.
Everyone says it will get better with time
But for me time hasn't been moving right.
I'm just stuck in the same place, living the same few days
Over and over and over again in my head.
I feel guilty for taking everything so personally
And bringing up past shit
When it seems like everyone else
Was moving on just fine until I opened the cracks again.
I feel guilty for always making things my problem
Instead of a collective experience.
I feel guilty on the days I don't cry;
I feel guilty for taking my medicine
Because why should I allow myself to get help,
To have the ability to focus on other shit now
When I promised you I'd hurt for you for the rest of my life?
I'm not better I'm just distracted,
Like feeling the buzz from a cup of alcohol
Can hide your problems for the night
But it's always worse the next morning.

I don't know if I'll be happy again;
I don't know if I'll ever let myself be.
Because moving on means forgetting
And I can't stand to lose you twice.

Brown Eyes

I'm envious of the girls with brown eyes.
The girls with cocoa and honey
Warming up and sweetening everyone
Who's lucky enough to be nearby.
They say that the eyes are the window to the soul
And there's something comforting
About the way a soul can be brown.
Yes, her eyes are blue like the depth of the ocean
And the sky after a storm has passed.
And yes, hers may be green like emeralds hidden underground
And leaves in a rainforest.
But oh darling,
Brown is like the root of every plant.
Brown is the dirt that brings life to everything on Earth.
Brown reminds me of the mountains
I dream of one day exploring.
It is in every season and every place called home;
The only thing that's constant in life.
Because the sky turns grey and purple and orange,
And the leaves turn red and fall to the ground,
But the trees remain brown year-round.
It is the color of strength, resilience, security, healing, fertility.
We are born symbolizing brown and we die returning to it.
The girls with eyes like these are beautiful
And they don't even have to try.
Sometimes the darkest colors
Are the ones more radiant than the sun.

Healing

I think healing is a lot like growing a plant.
Slow, frustrating, small changes at first.
But one day you wake up
And see that a flower has bloomed.
And before you know it
It's colorful and alive and thriving
Even if you never saw it making it past winter.
You have things that help nurture the growth.
And eventually you grow big and strong
And the rain doesn't destroy you,
It helps you turn into what you are supposed to be.
I think my first flower bloomed.
I think I am healing.

Freefalling

I never meant to fall for you, yet here we are,
Broken bones on the asphalt.
And I knew what I was getting into when I jumped,
But damn, the freefall was so fun.
No parachute, no mattress,
I for some reason trusted I'd land on my feet.
It was a bigger drop than I had presumed,
And it went too fast and then it was over just like that.
But it was exciting and it was new and it was scary all in one
And I'd honestly have half the mind to do it again
Just to feel the rush of it one more time
Because it hurt, but I'm not dead
And if you ask me, the best of it was worth the worst of it.
Half expecting you to catch me was a disappointment,
But still not a total letdown because I braced myself just in case.
I knew you'd take the elevator down instead
While I took a literal leap of faith,
Yet I was still willing to risk it all just to meet you at the bottom.
But when you saw me you walked away.
Didn't even bother to call me an ambulance
Or at least offer a hand to get me on my feet again.
It'd be stupid of me to walk back up as soon as the casts come off.
I've done stupid things before though.
Somehow I don't even think this was the stupidest thing I've done.
Sure, there's blood on the pavement
But the view was incredible from the top.

Fixed Hearts

I'm beginning to realize idolizing the past
Doesn't do anything to make the future better.
Thinking back then that this is as good as it gets
Is actually really depressing
Because it means that things will never be good again.
Much too often we think that once a heart breaks
The glue and tape we use to mend it
Won't ever make it heal to the way it was.
But our hearts aren't fine china or heavy mirrors,
They are human.
Humans can break their bones and be fine a few months later.
We can scrape our knees and forget it even happened.
Our bruises all fade, our cuts heal and only sometimes scar
But even the scars stop hurting after some time.
Your heart will break a thousand times if you're lucky
Because it means things kept getting good again
Even after you thought you were broken beyond repair.
Your past isn't as good as life can get,
It's just as good as it could've been right then.
Breathe.
You might need some bed rest
Or some medicine to help with the pain.
But one day you'll forget you even thought
Your heart wouldn't be happy again.

Wishes

I used all my birthday wishes on him.
Every dandelion ever blown,
Every eyelash that ever fell off,
Every shooting star that flashed across the sky.
It was all the same wish.
Magic happens if you dream of it long enough,
Though, sadly, insomnia keeps me wide awake.
All my wishes sat at the bottom of the well
Or were all used up on the person carrying the penny before.
My 11:11's were always caught a minute too late,
So maybe I just should've wished harder
To make up for the lost sleep and methods I couldn't use.
Maybe I should've found more flowers,
Plucked my eyelashes,
Drove out west where the sky looks endless.
I'm going to sleep tonight
And when I wake up I hope I see him.

Infinity

Infinity isn't real, at least not to us.
And maybe not even at all.
Because one day the Earth will stop spinning
And the sun will explode
And everything that once existed
Will cease to appear.
The only thing that might be infinite
Is the chain of reaction
Of finite occurrences.
Love will know no bounds
Until there's nothing else to love.
Still, that doesn't stop
Every summer from feeling endless.
It doesn't stop making me believe
That energy will always find a way
To bring us back to life.
And it doesn't stop me from thinking
That your eyes make time pause
For as long as I'm looking at them.
Everything has an end
Otherwise there would never be a start,
But maybe our infinities are real to us
Because in the little time we're here
The sun will always rise,
The sun will always set.

And maybe it's the feeling
Of never-ending hope that makes us try again.
Maybe it's the thought
That we aren't here forever that makes us try again.
We live, we die, that's the only thing that's promised.
We don't live forever in their hearts or their memories
Because three, four, five generations later
Will never hear about us again.
The point of life isn't "what's the point of life
If we're all just born to die."
The point of life is to live while we can
Because we're born to die.
If infinity isn't real
We need to search for it in everything we can
Before that disappears too.
Find your timeless love
Or your life-long passion
For whatever you want to do.
Everything that's real, and good, and worth it
Will make our infinities real to us.

The Silence

Often, I find that the best conversations
Are the ones never said out loud.
It's the silence that makes you realize
How truly comfortable you are with someone.
I'd be willing to sit by you at the lake all day,
Head on your shoulder,
Saying nothing but letting the breeze and the buzz
Do all the talking for itself.
Or sometimes it's not even about anyone else,
Just the conversations with yourself in your head.
I can learn a lot about myself
If I have the time to think.
And the mountains in Sante Fe
Made me realize more about life
Than I've ever learned in a classroom setting.
We all know that silence is the loudest scream,
But it's the gentle whispers too.
Bringing me my favorite drink after a hard day
And automatically turning on my favorite show
When I walk into your living room
Are things you never had to say out loud,
You just did it out of love.

45

Love is a puny word for itself anyway;
I can't find anything in the dictionary
That that adds up to the feelings I have.
Fondness, penchant, infatuated, besotted
Don't ever seem quite right.
So I love most in the silence.
Where a thousand words are spoken
Without ever opening my mouth.

A Ballad for Ronan

I'd give you the world if I could,
But my hands are much too small to hold it
And it would be improbable even if I could.
Instead, I'd tried to furnish you with a star once,
But quickly realized that I can only pinch them
From far away through my bedroom window.
You give me pieces of the sun with your warmth
And sand from the depths of the ocean
Just to prove that that's how deep your love goes,
But I seem to always come up empty-handed.
Even sunflowers seem to cut my hands like roses
From the guilt of presenting you with something so small.
And even now, the ink stains my fingers
As a reminder that my words are the only things I have to give.
These stupid, puny hands of mine
Cannot gather worlds or stars for you like I had hoped,
But at least they seem to fit snuggly inside of yours.

I'll Meet You at the Horizon

Know that I'll always meet you
At the horizon.
Where the water and the sky
Look like they're touching
But never are.
You were my favorite almost.
I got so wrapped up
In how I thought we were
A reflection of each other
That I didn't realize it was only one sided.
I based my beauty
On the way your light
Hit me just right,
On the way your colors
Seeped into my waves.
I don't think I have
Any effect on you
The way you did on me though.
And that realization
Hurt too much.
That's why I crash and roar
Onto the sand,
That's why I stay cold even in summer,
That's why I toss up broken shells
In my anger and my heartbreak.

Like twin flames,
Bound connect and touch
But hardly ever meant
To actually be together.
That's what we are.
So I still keep you
Close at a distance
And when it's time for you to go
Know I'll always meet you at the horizon.

Long Way Home

Tonight, I took the long way home
Because there's something more satisfying
About crying on the open road.
And whether it's the music
Blaring out my windows
Or the privacy of coming back
And no one will ever have to know,
I'm not sure.
Tonight, I played our song
Just to make it hurt again
And feel like I did back then,
When the hurt was fresh
And I thought we still had a chance,
But now it's been months
And I have to get over you.
I took the road that would take me to you
Without actually driving by your house
Because that would be crazy
And I don't want to be crazy
Unless I'm crazy for you again.
I thought of all the times
You rode shotgun in my car
Wishing you would hold my hand,
Instead, you were holding all the cards
To a game I didn't know anyway
So I never even had a chance.

Tonight, I drove to waste my gas
Because I don't have anything better to do.
My friends are busy drinking
'Cause they're used to me
Spending my time with you.
Tonight, I was tempted to crash into a tree
Because I just wanted to see
If after all this time and bad blood
You might still visit me.
I drove home instead.
I sat in my car for hours
Thinking I was dead
Because I was convinced my heart
Had stopped beating at that point.
I drove the long way home
Without actually driving anywhere
Except for driving myself crazy.
Backroads are meant
For the people living in their head,
Not the ones actually trying to get somewhere.
And as I'm thinking about this
Back in my driveway where I belong,
I collapse into a million pieces
Inside of myself
Wondering where we all went wrong.
Tonight, I took the long way home
And kind of half-hoped
You were taking that road too.

Amaris

I don't believe in angels, but if I did
I'd imagine they'd be like her.
Soft words echo past her lips
And dance in the air
Before they make it to your ears.
It's like she has sugar on her tongue
And can't help but say the sweetest things.
She is Heaven if I've ever seen it.
Not perfect, but something to be in awe of.
Her beauty bound to no human words.
Ethereal, light as if air were to move through her.
I caught her smiling at me once
And I've seen colors ever since.

Estranged

My journal knows your name,
Each letter engraved through the pages
Until it knew no other words.
Everything that's mine
Is familiar with you.
My pillow knows who hurt me
Because I cursed your name into it
And wiped my tears on the same side.
The cushion you sat in so often
Has not yet retaken its shape;
It's as if it's planning on seating you again.
I've pulled blinds over every window
Because they're not used
To the reflection of just my face.
Becoming estranged to you
Is becoming estranged to my life.
I do not know how to go
From a home to a house
When I'd waited my whole life
To finally have a place to call home.
No, these walls aren't cracking;
No, the floor isn't caving,
But my home was never defined
By walls and a floor,

Home was what I wanted to come back to
At the end of every day.
You were my home.
And this house knows you,
My body knows you.
You've left a ghost of yourself
By the front door
Mocking us when I go inside.
"Here I am, in everything but presence.
If you can't keep me,
I will make sure you can never get rid of me,"
It whispers in my ear.
Waiting, challenging me
To burn the whole place down
Until the only thing that knows you
Is what I carry in my head.

Untitled III

My life feels like waiting on a train.
And no, I don't mean getting passed by in the station,
In some ways I think that'd be better.
I mean I'm sitting on a train,
Watching others get on and off
While I stay still in my seat.
I'm looking out the window
Waiting to see the wonders
Of my new destination
But I can't find it because I don't know what it looks like.
You see, this whole time I thought I was going somewhere,
Was running to something,
But I wasn't moving at all.
The train was just carrying me where it was headed.
It's an optical illusion, you see,
Thinking you're going somewhere
While really life is just passing you by.

Peaches

Remember what it was like
To be young and gripping on
To the edges of summer,
Begging for it not to end quite yet?
The afternoons spent
Getting sand caught
In your sun-bleached hair.
The morning sunrises
After you stayed up all night
Because your body
Was too busy bursting with energy
Instead of focusing on sleep.
That night spent eating cherries
Though he said
They tasted like peaches.
I want to pull those summers
Up to my chin like a blanket
And let it wrap me up,
Warm and soft
Like it was back then.
Still gripping onto the edges,
Afraid of when winter will come
And snatch it all away.

To My Younger Self

If I were to tell my younger self anything,
I'd tell her I'm still here,
But not in the way that I haven't
Lost myself to suicide,
In the way that I'm still real.
I feel detached to her right now,
As if seeing her through a screen
Like a projector of a movie
That I've hardly ever seen.
She is still me.
Her thoughts not in my brain,
I say it's 'cause I've changed,
I say it's 'cause I feel detached
From the way I've been attacked.
It's as if her life didn't happen to me
And I just appeared one day
To take her place.
I would tell her to never let others
Convince her her dreams are too big for this world.
I've lost sight of them lately
And I haven't been the same since.
Since I lost track of which track I was following.
Since I've felt this gut feeling inside of me hollowing.
Since I've taken things I shouldn't be swallowing.

I'm hardly doing anything but wallowing
In self pity since common sense
Went out the window.
But what do I know?
It's just my two cents.
I want to warn her that "better" doesn't mean "good."
Maybe she'd stop expecting so much
If she knew the limits between
What should and what could.
And I want to remind her while I'm at it,
She's not crazy, just misunderstood.
Somewhere deep inside of me
If I peel back enough layers
I can find her crying herself to sleep,
And I'll whisper in her ear,
"This pain isn't yours to keep."
I'd take it all away from her
If only given the chance,
But shoving it all down
Has only left me in a trance.
I'd hug her when she needed,
Calm her nerves and make her tea.
I'd try to tell her she's still here
But I am not her and she is not me.

A Poem About Breathing

I feel it coming again—
Pins and needles in my face,
My lungs contracting,
My body caving in on itself
As I'm fighting the urge
To cry, to scream, to panic.
My breaths are so shallow
I can still see my feet
As I'm wading in my thoughts,
Yet they are heavy and loud
Like a boulder crushed my ribs.
My lips have gone numb.
Is it from using my mouth
Too much all of a sudden
From trying to gasp in air
Or is it just the pins and needles
Have found their way there?
Everything is shaky:
My legs, my hands, my breathing.
One—Focusfocusfocusfocusfocus.
This is a moment, it will pass.
Two—Concentrate on the other person
In the room or something you can hold.
Three—In, hold it, out, hold it.

59

Four—Repeat until your chest
Has opened some.
Five—Touch your face.
Remind yourself you are not
Made of static.
Six—Breathe.
Again.
Again.

Again.

Fate

I think Aphrodite got it wrong.
Found you in the verse to every song.
I thought your chest was my bed
And the place where I belonged.

Heaven knows I thought the stars aligned,
Forgot that stars stay moving all the time.
But for just one second, please don't end it,
For a moment the Gods called us divine.

I'd spent a lifetime inside our six months,
Still not ready to give it all up.
I'll say I'm fine with too much leftover time.
How can I live with only having you once?

I think Aphrodite's laughing in the clouds
Just can't wait to rip our hearts out.
I've returned it, but I can't unlearn it.
She said it's the only outcome that's allowed.

I'm the version of myself who didn't try hard enough;
Guess you're the version that was too scared to fall in love.
Those shooting stars last night were just our souls falling from the
    sky
Without a warning, we were fine 'til we got shoved.

I caught her conspiring with the Gods of fate.
Tried to defend my case but I got there too late.
Story goes we wrecked it; sealed it in an epic.
Apparently our lives weren't up for debate.

There's no avoiding what's written in the sky.
Destined to be lovers but not for life.
If we knew what we know now, wouldn't feel so let down.
Wouldn't have followed Icarus up so high.

But if those stars ever drift close together again,
Not sure how and not sure when,
Know I'd want to be called yours and reopen these closed doors.
I'll be praying for the day you walk back in.

Untitled IV

62

I'm not sure which has seen me at my worst—
My bathroom and bedroom
Have been through it all with me.
But it was when I collapsed on the living room floor
That I knew my sadness truly consumed me.
And all the pillowcases and toilet paper in the world
Could not save me from that moment.

Best Friends

We started to have sleepovers
About once or twice a month
And I got scared that meant
We were losing touch.
I started reminiscing
Back when we were
12 and basically
Lived in each other's houses.
Those were the days
We were inseparable
And talked about
Almost nothing but boy bands
And what kind of dreams
We had planned for our lives.
We never called each other
By our names,
Instead just reverted to
"Best Friend."
And how sad I am now
That you're not
Right across the street
And we answer
The phone calls
With our first names.

My first tattoo
Was in honor of you,
The person I'd known
Since we were 8.
I barely have memories
Before you.
Then I thought about
How I still refer to you
As my "bestie"
When I introduce
You to all my new friends.
Now I'm lying in
Your bed beside you
And it hits me
That this love we have
And time apart
Makes our relationship
Feel more like
A sisterly bond.
I could spill my life to you
For the rest of my life
And I can't picture
Our wedding days
Where we are not
The maids of honor.

You are whom
I always go back to;
Without question
The person who knows
They are always invited
To every special event.
How much do you
Have to know someone,
How deeply do you have
To love someone
In order to feel
Like they are
Truly family?